Pathways to Devotion III
By Linda McBurney-Gunhouse

Published by:
Creative Focus Publishing
Winnipeg Beach, Manitoba, Canada

Cover Artwork by Linda McBurney-Gunhouse
ISBN: 978-1-928071-15-0

Copyright © 2007 by Linda McBurney-Gunhouse
All Rights Reserved.
R7

Published by:
Creative Focus Publishing
Box 704
Winnipeg Beach, Manitoba
R0C 3G0 CANADA

Please visit our website:
www.creativefocus.ca

Contact us at:
info@creativefocus.ca

All Scripture is taken from the King James Version of the Bible, unless otherwise stated.

A Note from the Author

Pathways to Devotion III, similar to the first two books, promises new and insightful inspirational reflections to encourage you as you journey along through life's many interesting pathways. Backed by spiritual themes, you'll find quotes from the Bible in each reflection, designed to uplift, strengthen and create pause for thought.

Many of the reflections are little stories of interesting, insightful and even miraculous things that have happened to me through the years. Underlying it all is a faith in a loving God who promises He will be with us throughout all the circumstances of life. At the end of each reflection, is a section called Application. Here, you are given a guideline for further Scripture reading, prayer and further reflection. I invite you to use this book as a companion to your Bible and treat it as either a daily devotional book, or use it as a guideline for small Bible study groups. I leave you with one of my favourite passages of Scripture:

Psalm 23:1-3,6

The LORD is my shepherd; I shall not want. He maketh me to lie down in green pastures: he leadeth me beside the still waters. He restoreth my soul: he leadeth me in the paths of righteousness for his name's sake. Surely goodness and mercy shall follow me all the days of my life: and I will dwell in the house of the LORD forever.

Linda McBurney-Gunhouse
Winnipeg Beach, MB
Canada

Contents

Day 1 - Doing the Right Thing 1
Day 2 - Meeting the Prime Minister 3
Day 3 - About Keys 5
Day 4 - A Different View 7
Day 5 - Respect of Persons 9
Day 6 - A 100-Fold Return 11
Day 7 - Who Do We Follow? 13
Day 8 - Contentment 15
Day 9 - God's Prescription 17
Day 10 - Paying the Price 19
Day 11 - Whose Ship? 21
Day 12 - Dream Source 23
Day 13 - Overcoming Trials 25
Day 14 - Blurred Vision 27
Day 15 - Making Resolutions 29
Day 16 - Gardening in All Seasons 31
Day 17 - A Comforting Psalm 33
Day 18 - Getting Good News 35
Day 19 - Hand-Me Downs 37
Day 20 - Mount St. Helens 39
Day 21 - Being Stedfast 41
Day 22 - Survival Guide 43
Day 23 - Color Your World 45
Day 24 - Serving or Solicitation? 47
Day 25 - Simplicity 49
Day 26 - The Challenger 51
Day 27 - A Furry Alarm Clock 53
Day 28 - Once is Enough 55
Day 29 - Giants in the Land 57
Day 30 - Confidence 59
Day 31 - What Kind of Memories? 61
An Invitation for Salvation 63
About the Author 64
Other Titles 66

This book is lovingly dedicated to the memory of Marguerite Eleanor Gunhouse, my mother-in-law, who went home to heaven March 3, 2007. She was a lovely woman who lived well and loved well.

Day 1 - <u>Doing the Right Thing</u>

That ye might walk worthy of the Lord unto all pleasing, being fruitful in every good work, and increasing in the knowledge of God; Strengthened with all might, according to his glorious power, unto all patience and longsuffering with joyfulness; Colossians 1:10-11

One mild winter day I went for my daily walk to clear my thoughts and also enjoy the fresh winter air. Feeling somewhat discouraged from some financial setbacks typical to the slower winter season and sensing a quietness in my life that seemed to draw a curtain of loneliness around me, the Lord had a chance to speak to me.

I was thinking about other people — how everyone I knew or knew of seemed to be busy, going here and there, working, attending events, and lost in the wonderful busyness of life, enjoying themselves, while I seemed to be stuck in a rut with nowhere to go. The Lord, rather than condemn me for entertaining such self-introspective thoughts, encouraged me when He said that I was actually living a life that was pleasing to Him because even though it was difficult, I was doing the right thing. I was following my convictions, and pursuing the tasks He had placed in my heart (such as writing inspirational books). That even though it was difficult for me to stay put and write, edit and publish these books myself, that it was the right thing for me to do, because these are my deepest convictions, something that I know I must complete.

Parents who are sacrificing their time for the worthy job of raising their children may also feel this way at times, that life is passing them by, as they get caught up in the many involvements of raising their children. Yet, what a rewarding task — raising children that will one day also see your sacrifice of time and treat their children with the same love and care. Still others may be busy in their life, but not satisfied, so spend their time searching for meaning and purpose in an otherwise purposeless day-to-day existence.

As well, when I went for that walk I was reminded that when all is said and done, it shouldn't matter to me as much what other people do and don't do, as it does what I do with this life that God has freely and graciously given me. I am only responsible for me. Far more than just seek fulfillment or the "balanced" and perfect life we sometimes pressure ourselves to lead, I need to be more concerned that at the end of each day I have done my best to follow the Lord's leading and direction in my life.

How easy it is to become discontent and forget that we are on this earth mainly for spiritual purposes, not to please our own selves and appease the "flesh" or live for our own "self" life. Sometimes we can put more emphasis on this than completing our God-given tasks at hand. When we come to the end of our days, how wonderful to know that we have done our absolute best to live a life based on doing the right thing rather than a life that simply pleased our flesh.

Application

Read: 2 Timothy 4:1-8

Pray: That God will lead, guide and direct you each day to complete the work He has for you to do, so that you may do the right thing that is pleasing to Him.

Reflect: What does doing the right thing mean for you? Write it down and then begin today to take a step towards doing the right thing.

Day 2 - <u>Meeting the Prime Minister</u>

Beloved, now are we the sons of God, and it doth not yet appear what we shall be: but we know that, when he shall appear, we shall be like him; for we shall see him as he is. 1 John 3:2

Several years ago when I was a journalism student in college, I had the privilege of meeting the then Prime Minister Pierre Trudeau. Since our journalism class was practicing interviewing techniques for press conferences, we had the honor of being able to ask Mr. Trudeau specific questions we had devised and then later write a news report on the press conference. Although I never had the opportunity to ask him questions directly, I did have the opportunity to meet him face to face. I shook his hand and he greeted me and smiled. I was very impressed with his friendliness and that even though he had such a high position, he still took time for the public, even young and inexperienced journalists like myself. I had only seen Mr. Trudeau in the paper and also on TV many times. His charisma was sweeping the headlines as he made many important international connections and contributed to raising the status of Canada from back-woods to a larger country ready to do business with the world. I was surprised that although he was a big man politically, he was actually physically quite a small man.

This encounter with our Prime Minister (at the time) had a big impact on me in many other ways. Meeting him in person and having shared this delightful hour or so with him (he had a wonderful sense of humor), made me realize that people in high positions of power are just human like the rest of us. They have exactly the same needs, for when our press conference was over, it was lunch time. While we went to the college cafeteria, Mr. Trudeau was whisked off to some elaborate private luncheon probably with the governor general or premier of our province. He also had to eat.

Day 2

A few years later, it hit me that I am also going to see Jesus face to face. The magnitude of this thought still astounds me and I can't quite comprehend it all, the God of the whole universe and all things created, who judges the living and the dead and all living persons, and knows us each by name. All that we have heard about Him and read about Him and the little bit that we know about Him will be fully realized when we finally see Him face to face. And how will this be possible? This is even more astounding — 1 John 4:2 (see opening verse) says that **when he shall appear, we shall be like him.** How else could we see Him and understand Him except we be like Him?

We may have met the Prime Minister, the Queen of England, the President of the United States or a host of other high-up officials, but we haven't even begun to touch greatness until we see the Lord Jesus face-to-face, for He is the One who loves us and gave His life for us. Some day we will all see Him face-to-face, including kings, queens, presidents and prime ministers, rich and poor, servants and masters. This is where we are all at the same level with titles stripped, and crowns tossed away, and see ourselves for who we really are. And if we know Him, we will be like Him — an awesome thought!

Application

Read: Revelation 22:1-14

Pray: for all those in authority over us, especially that they will one day be ready to meet the Lord Jesus face to face.

Reflect: Are you ready to meet Jesus face to face? Think about it and write about it. If you are not ready, what will you do today to be ready?

Day 3 - <u>About Keys</u>

And I will give unto thee the keys of the kingdom of heaven: and whatsoever thou shalt bind on earth shall be bound in heaven: and whatsoever thou shalt loose on earth shall be loosed in heaven.
Matthew 16:19

Have you ever accidentally left your car keys in the ignition, locked the car and had to find a way to either pry open a slightly open window with a coat hanger, or finally give up and call the garage or a motor vehicle emergency road service to open the door? I sure have. When I worked at the university, I had absent-mindedly left the keys in my van more than a few times. Seeing the CAA tow truck come through the large parking lot became a familiar occurrence and an embarrassing one.

Other times, I have forgotten my mail key to open the post office box. The mail man has been kind enough to hand me the mail, but still it's an inconvenience. I've also dropped my house keys to the ground since there is a gap between the deck and our house. Again, I've had to fish them out with a long bent coat hanger. Or sometimes I set them down and can't remember where I left them. I've often found them in my coat pocket instead of my purse.

Too many keys can be a nuisance, too, because the more you have, the likelier you are to lose them. Plus they can really weigh you down if you carry too many around. For instance, I have keys for my suitcases, the shed doors, locks for the camper, the lattice fence doors in the back yard that my husband built, and I carry around other keys that I don't even know what they're for anymore! When we lived in the city, I had to carry around a whole other set of keys for our apartment, which I also lost in a snow bank in a parking lot and had to have them all replaced from my husband's set! It gets even more confusing if I use more than one purse, or

Day 3

if I drive my husband's car instead of my van.

One day I was thinking about keys and how much stress and trouble they have caused me even though I know they are necessary because we live in a fallen world where there are dishonest people and thieves will look for opportunities to steal. Then something else came to mind. I thought about the spiritual application and use of keys as in the opening verse. The Lord has actually given us a great gift — the keys to the kingdom of heaven! He didn't say "earth." He said, "heaven." So what do we do with these keys and what is the significance of this ability? I believe that we can actually open and close doors in the spiritual realm with these spiritual keys. Through prayer we can close doors where evil might try to enter in, and we can also release God's will (according to His Word) to prevail on earth as it is in heaven. This is also implied in the Lord's Prayer. God's will is released on this earth when we pray — that's a powerful thought! We can actually prevent evil by prayer and set in motion the Lord's will instead.

Like a car that can't start and a house door that won't open without a key, God's will is often accomplished on this earth through the powerful gift of prayer. May we use these keys often and wisely!

<u>Application</u>

<u>Read</u>: Luke 11:2-4,9-10

<u>Pray</u>: Use your spiritual keys and pray for God's specific will in any situation that comes to mind. Ask for God's guidance as you seek to use these keys.

<u>Reflect</u>: Write out your thoughts about the opening verse. Act on what it says to do.

Day 4 - <u>A Different View</u>

And we know that all things work together for good to them that love God, to them who are the called according to his purpose. Romans 8:28

For many years when I lived in the city I lived in an apartment. I always hoped I would one day own a house because then I wouldn't have to worry about rent going up every year, and I'd be able to decorate it or change it and do whatever I pleased with it. But best of all, I'd have my own yard instead of a small cement patio overlooking a busy highway or other apartments. Being an outdoor person and an artist, environment and scenery are important to me and I like a view that inspires me.

After I got married, my husband and I did buy a house in a resort area (actually we're considered an independent town situated in a provincial park) about one hour north of the city. The town is situated right beside one of the largest inland freshwater lakes in the world, Lake Winnipeg. You can imagine how beautiful it is in the summer, with the sunrise every morning and moonrise every evening.

As lovely as our surroundings are, every fall we witness a wind storm. The lake is shallow so when wind hits the water, waves can be as high as 20 feet in some places. One year a fierce wind storm took down several tall Jack pine trees all throughout the area and we lost power for several hours. Some of our neighbours trees went down in this storm. We also had two 80 foot high Jack pine trees in our backyard (the only trees there). Although they provided shade and some privacy, every year a wind storm would come up and they would sway so violently we wondered when or if they would snap and fall, perhaps on the electrical wires connecting our main power source to the house. So we finally hired a tree-cutter to cut them down. I had no idea how difficult this would be because it completely changed the view and I had a hard time adjusting because now our back yard was partially exposed with no more privacy from the trees. I grieved over losing these trees. But after a few days I noticed the benefits. The trees were on the south side, so all winter we would have bright hot sun in the office where we work, and this would lower our heating bills. I also noticed the many trees beyond and the quaint rooftops of other nearby cottages. My husband had a wider area to park his car. And we felt much safer. Every time there is a wind storm, we no longer worry that our trees might fall and injure someone or fall on our house.

I am reminded of the verse in Romans 8:28 — that even though we might feel a loss when we lose something (yes, even trees), there are always benefits to be gained once we stop seeing what we're missing and start seeing what we've gained (or still have). God has promised that ALL THINGS work together for good, even when it seems like they won't. Many times when things seem the darkest, this is when God shines His light the brightest. For me, at first I noticed the absence of our trees, but soon I noticed the bright beautiful fall sun beaming through all my south windows, warming my heart and my long winter days. May you also find the good in your losses however big or small.

Application

Read: Psalm 92

Pray: for God to help you see the benefits through any loss you may feel or a change you are not yet comfortable with. Pray for someone today who is also feeling a loss.

Reflect: How can we grow through change of circumstance and also through loss? Journal about a loss you've had and how you coped with it. Share this with someone who needs a friend.

Day 5 - <u>Respect of Persons</u>

But the LORD said unto Samuel, Look not on his countenance, or on the height of his stature; because I have refused him: for the LORD seeth not as man seeth; for man looketh on the outward appearance, but the LORD looketh on the heart. 1 Samuel 16:7

    One summer my family all met in my home town for its 125th Anniversary celebrations. What a great time of reunion we had. The organizers of this event-filled week-long celebration, offered pancake breakfasts every morning and each evening different companies or organizations hosted supper, which was offered in a different location. This is where we met many old friends and acquaintances that we hadn't seen in several years. There were lots of hugs, laughter and even some tears, mostly of joy, and other times of sadness. There were also school reunions all week which brought together many of our school friends.

    Growing up in this quaint town with its winding river, huge park, town hill, valleys, creek, and lots of trees, we were a close-knit community, even though the population boasted of 2,000 residents. Everyone knows everyone and it is hard to keep a secret for very long before the whole town knows about it. For instance, when my sister and I were teenagers, we might take the family car and drive around town even though my dad hadn't given us permission to. Sure enough, someone my dad knows would see us and call my dad, and then we'd be sorry for what we did when we got home.

    But there were some secrets that I never knew about until they were revealed that week of the 125th Anniversary and even after that. I'm sure they weren't intended to be secrets, but in some cases, were more like answered prayers. All the while growing up, our small church had been faithfully praying for the community. And now, I was able to see just how far those prayers had gone. I was surprised to discover, for example, that one of my sister's schoolmates had become a big business owner, owning a well-known franchise of a restaurant known world-wide. But more than this, he shared that he had just bought a Christian radio station. Then I discovered that after he left home, he met a girl that led him to the Lord (and he later married) and he and his wife have been active Christians in their community all these years. Then about three months later, a former schoolmate I had been reacquainted with during our school reunion, called me and asked if we could meet for coffee in a nearby city. I was hoping to witness to her, but she ended up witnessing to me when she told me that she was studying to become an ordained minister and that she and her husband were involved in missions.

What struck me about these two instances is that we need to keep praying for people, even if it takes years to see results. My sister's schoolmate not only came to the Lord, but is now reaching thousands and even millions of people via the radio airwaves. My friend from school is preaching from the pulpit and involved in missions that will also reach people world-wide. These are two people I would never have thought would even become a Christian. While it is easy to give up on people when they seem least likely to respond to the Gospel, we must never pre-judge anyone and think that they wouldn't be interested in Christianity, when they may be the next Billy Graham! May we be open to the Lord's leading and keep on praying!

Application

Read: 2 Corinthians 4:1-7

Pray: for people God lays on your heart. Pray for courage to witness and that God would lead you to lost souls.

Reflect: When you became a Christian, who witnessed to you? Go and do the same for someone God lays on your heart.

Day 6 - <u>A 100-Fold Return</u>

Cast thy bread upon the waters: for thou shalt find it after many days. Ecclesiastes 11:1

When I first started putting these devotional books together, I was excited about sharing little stories about what the Lord had taught me, stories that I had written even years earlier. I had always kept a journal and every time something significant happened, I'd write it down. Through the years, I would often re-read to remind me of God's faithfulness and also to encourage me in my faith. However, in publishing them myself, I discovered the great cost, both in time and also financial resources. But both my husband and I felt that the books are also a means of ministry much more than the marketing of them. So we agreed to give them away when the Lord directed us to do so.

After awhile I noticed that we were giving away more than we were actually selling and could no longer even cover our costs for printing them. So I took it up in prayer before the Lord. Rather than provide a financial means to mass-produce them at a lower cost, He instead said that it would produce fruit in people's lives and also He promised me 100-fold for each book that I gave away. That very day when I went to get the mail, there was a substantial cheque from a relative who had only bought a couple of books, but was donating the rest "for ministry." How could he have known what the Lord was trying to teach me?

There have been times my husband and I have thought that maybe we should apply for a charities number and register under a charity name so that people will feel more comfortable in giving to our ministry, or even to donate something towards the books, since then they would get a tax receipt. But we felt this would in some way rob people of an even greater blessing when they give expecting nothing

Day 6

(from the world or the government) in return. We believe people would receive a much greater return from the hand of the Lord, much more than a human institution offers.

In our own life, we have seen the Lord supernaturally provide for us countless times in ways that are unimaginable from a natural perspective. This has made our giving exciting and rewarding as we see God's promises return to us time and again. Sometimes we receive financial reward; other times we see our vehicle carry us for many miles without even needing repair. And often He surprises us with much more than we even asked for.

So often we look to the world to provide an answer for our needs. This is easier than listening to the voice of God and then believing Him and obeying what He says. For me to give away books I've poured my heart and life into stretches me in my faith, but I know God sees it and He will provide what I need when I need it. When we choose the world's way, we will only receive back what the world promises. So if I put $1,000 in the bank, I might get 1 or 2% interest. That's all I'm going to get back. But if I give that same $1,000 to God' work, I will receive 100-fold in return, much more than the bank offers. It makes us pause in our giving, and even ask ourselves, "Are we giving to get a tax receipt back?" Or "Are we giving to further God's work, expecting nothing (from the world or the government) in return?" May we always give with the right motives and expect 100-fold from God's limitless resources.

Application

<u>Read</u>: Ecclesiastes 11

<u>Pray</u>: **For God to reveal your heart when it comes to giving. Ask Him to show you where He wants you to give.**

<u>Reflect</u>: **When are some times you have given and God has blessed you above and beyond what you expected? Write about it.**

Day 7 - <u>Who Do We Follow?</u>

And he said to them all, If any man will come after me, let him deny himself, and take up his cross daily, and follow me. Luke 9:23

One late fall, as my thoughts were turning towards Christmas and all the preparations necessary to make it a memorable occasion, I was struck by the thought of busyness itself and what it actually produces. For everything we do, there are results and consequences — sometimes good, sometimes bad and sometimes nothing. We can actually be ruled by a busy schedule, and only realize it when we start to feel burned out. If this is the case, we have taken a wrong turn somewhere and need to get back on track. And I clearly saw this in spiritual terms because of the many years I spent researching the topic of backsliding and discovered that the world in which we live can profoundly influence our level of busyness.

As a young teenager, I must confess, that much of my busyness was just for the sake of having fun and, often getting myself into some kind of trouble. Without meaningful employment or even helping out with chores at home, many youth fall into the snares of the world and the devil. And peer pressure is the greatest at this age, as teens strive to fit in with the "in" crowd. For young Christians in a public school, standing up for the Lord can be a very difficult thing because it seems to them that what others think is greater than what the Lord thinks of us. But for every age group, there is always the temptation to follow the latest fads and fashions of the world, and chase after what everyone else is. Even church involvements can amount to a lot of empty busyness when we're asked to do things for the sake of a social event. While social events are enjoyable and even necessary at times, they should never take precedence over more important busy work that the Lord's kingdom requires of us, such as lots of prayer and then Spirit-led

Day 7

outreach to the lost.

In my own life I have been called "out of the world" both sometimes physically (at least temporarily) and spiritually (positionally for all believers in Christ according to John 15:19), so I have been able to discern the times I have been busy without good cause and the times I have been busy doing the work of the Lord. But it hasn't always been easy to make choices, when I could have been out on a shopping frenzy, going to movies and so on, and instead staying home to complete something of a lesser social nature, like researching and writing.

But one thing I have learned is that the world is an unsteady, unpredictable place to live. Fashions, fads, and popular people come and go more often than ever. If we follow after the things of the world, we will be tossed, torn and disappointed time and again as the results we had hoped for leave us empty, unsatisfied and stressed out in the end. Jesus has called us to follow Him — what an exciting thought! He promises peace, rest and safety, not to mention all the many adventures in faith that He will introduce us to along the way. We'll always come away refreshed, blessed, filled with encouragement, and a new resolve to do more for the Lord. The cost? We deny the temporary pleasures of the world and instead discover the freedom and joy in walking with the Lord.

Application

Read: Luke 9:23-26; 1 Timothy 6:10-12

Pray: For God to help you be able to discern what you should be doing and what you should avoid doing. Do this daily.

Reflect: Other than your work, what do you spend your time doing? Re-focus where needed and make a new schedule where you include more you can do for the Lord.

Day 8 - <u>Contentment</u>

Not that I speak in respect of want: for I have learned, in whatsoever state I am, therewith to be content. Philippians 4:11

Although we live in a beautiful quiet resort area, my husband has had to drive an hour to and from work in the city every day. When his office was transferred, it added an extra half hour each way. Over the years, and especially after the transfer, from time to time we would consider renting an apartment in the city at least in the late fall and winter months, to reduce his driving time. Some of the apartments were old and shabby, yet still they were asking a considerable amount for the rent. I would always come home and look around our cozy, window-filled house and thank God for providing such a wonderful bright and cheerful place to live.

In fact I remember when we first bought the house — the thrill of living only a five minute walk to the lake, the trees on our property, the peaceful quietness when all the cottagers went back to the city for the winter, our own private back yard and my first attempt at gardening. A place of rest and quiet reflection, perfect for writing and reading, relaxing and also inviting friends and family for barbecues, art shows and visits, this house has indeed been a blessing from God.

Yet some winters have been more challenging than others, especially when one winter we went from two vehicles to one, which meant I would have no way to go out and even go uptown to get the mail as I usually did. To add to my discouragement, a few people I knew were going on fabulous holidays to exotic places, and I felt stuck at home, with not even the slightest chance of being able to go anywhere. Even though I had stacks of work to do and writing to catch up on, still, I longed for a chance to be able to get out. Yet, what was I going to do? I had two choices — either I would mope around and feel sorry

Day 8

for myself, or I would accept my circumstances and believe that God knew my heart's desires and my needs, and that He had my best interests at heart. I chose the latter and then received the gift of complete contentment of just being at home, to the point that I almost felt sorry for the people who had gone away on a holiday because they would eventually have to come home and face reality again. But I was already living in my reality and things started looking pretty wonderful as I began to see God's many blessings He had already provided. I came to realize that God had already provided me with His best and I didn't need anything more. I could be content with my life as it already is.

Shortly after this, God provided another miracle. We discovered we were financially able to purchase a condo in the city only eight minutes from my husband's work. And not just any condo — it had everything we could have hoped for including three bedrooms, two bathrooms, and 200 more square feet than even our house has. And we still were able to keep our house!

Discontentment is something to avoid at all costs because it blinds us to the blessings we already have. I realized that if we had bought the condo while I was still discontent with my life at the house, eventually I likely wouldn't have been content with the condo either. Contentment is one of God's greatest gifts — may we covet it and treasure it when we have it.

Application

<u>Read</u>: Philippians 4:11-13

<u>Pray</u>: For God to give you an extra measure of contentment if you feel discontent for any reason.

<u>Reflect</u>: Think of a time you felt complete contentment. What happened? Are you content now? Is so, write about it and explain why. Share your blessings with someone today.

Day 9 - <u>God's Prescription</u>

Do not be anxious about anything, but in everything, by prayer and petition, with thanksgiving, present your requests to God. And the peace of God, which transcends all understanding, will guard your hearts and your minds in Christ Jesus.
Philippians 4:6-7 NIV

Recently I read that the pharmaceutical industry in Canada is worth over 21 billion dollars. And if that isn't big enough, add the medications available in your local grocery and drug store shelves that are filled with every kind of medication imaginable, for colds, headaches, general pain, arthritis, allergies and so on. As a person ages, more and more drugs are prescribed for various ailments to try and keep the body healthy and functioning properly. And since the main population in Canada is an aging one, the drug industry will top even the 21 billion dollar mark.

While we can be very thankful for medications that do help us, drugs can only do so much. Sometimes doctors don't always know the best medication to prescribe and so can't help a person. And some people, like me, have drug reactions that are worse than the actual ailment. Some people become addicted to their medications and feel they can't get along without them, such as sleeping pills and other drugs that relax the body.

I believe that many ailments, other than diseases caused by generational gene weaknesses, are created in the first place from worry, stress, anger and a host of things that put incredible stress on our emotional, mental and physical selves. In many cases, when taking medication for stress, drugs only mask the problem and never really get to the root cause of the problem. In my own case, many years ago, just after I had moved from my home town to the big city, I had a very difficult time adjusting to my new surroundings. I

Day 9

would often wake up in the middle of the night from nightmares that I couldn't shake, and so finally I went for some counseling. My problem was diagnosed as fear, but no amount of medication could remove the fear, because fear has a spiritual root. It also seemed to me that fear and anxiety would sneak up on me and I felt powerless to deal with either one. Many years later, I realized that fear was a demonic force and anxiety was a result of me believing the lies Satan was whispering in my ear. I also discovered a battle plan that worked, and it had nothing to do with any prescribed medication. Instead, I literally took God's Word and verbally used it as my greatest weapon by quoting the verses that oppose fear and anxiety. Pretty soon the nightmares stopped and so did the almost constant state of anxiety that I couldn't seem to shake.

Many people accept their illnesses, fears and stresses as a natural part of life, and so in a very real sense, remain dependent on the drug industry to keep them going. But I believe God made us in such a way that our best answer is only found in Him and His Word. Once we accept Jesus as our Lord and personal Savior, He becomes our Doctor and our Healer, our Counselor and our Friend. We can depend on Him and no matter what state our physical or emotional health is in, He promises us peace if we turn everything over to Him.

Application

Read: Philippians 4:6-9; 2 Timothy 1:7

Pray: for God to reveal any areas of your life that need His special touch. Ask God to help you overcome any non life-threatening drug dependencies and set you free to trust in Him instead.

Reflect: When are the times you have felt the most peace? Write about it and then repeat what you did then to experience peace again.

Day 10 - <u>Paying the Price</u>

For all have sinned, and come short of the glory of God; Being justified freely by his grace through the redemption that is in Christ Jesus: Romans 3:23-24

Have you ever heard someone talk about how hard they've worked to earn something and then take credit for their accomplishments? I sure have, and I'm sure I've done the same more than a few times. Someone might take credit for working hard to pay off their mortgage, or pay off a loan for a new car, or pay for their education. Retired people take credit for working for 25 or 30 years and how they've paid the price for their leisurely time off. I have even heard parents say that by having kids and raising them, they have done their duty and paid their price to society. People take credit for losing weight, getting in shape, quitting smoking or drinking and staying on the straight and narrow. We believe that our hard work earns us a reward and it is our right.

While this is partly true that we've earned a reward, since even the Bible says in Matthew 10:10, that "the worker is worthy of his meat," there are other issues to consider. When we give ourselves too much credit for our accomplishments, this amounts to self-congratulatory pride. Pride, while it temporarily builds us up, can make others feel inferior or like failures. This is no way negates the need to feel a healthy pride of our accomplishments, since this is often what spurs us on to the next big accomplishment. But we must be careful to turn our good success outward, so that others truly benefit and God gets the praise and glory and not ourselves. The Bible talks about "encouraging one another daily" (see Hebrew 3:13) and that we need to be building each other up so that we are "always abounding in the work of the Lord" (see 1 Cor. 15:58). I believe God blesses us so that we can bless others. For example, if God blesses me with a big house, then He must intend me to use

Day 10

a gift of hospitality and invite others over for meals, a Bible Study, or even a place to stay. Or if He blesses us with a bigger pay cheque, then He is trusting us to tithe more than we do now.

Also, the idea of taking personal credit for our accomplishments really flies in the face of Scripture, since Jesus completely paid the price for our salvation and granted us eternal life. His price? His own life!! This means that we belong to Him and everything else does as well — all our possessions, our dreams, our future and our accomplishments. Everything belongs to Him to use according to His will. An even more convicting thought — would we be willing to work for 25 or 30 years so that someone else may enjoy our retirement years even though they haven't worked for one day to earn that time off? Or if we worked hard to pay off our mortgage and car loan, would we give our house and car to someone else with no strings attached even though they hadn't contributed one penny? This all sounds ludicrous, yet when Jesus died for us, He paid the TOTAL BILL OF OUR DEBT WITH NO STRINGS ATTACHED!!! The very least we should do is give Him credit for all our blessings and be willing to give it all back to Him, and also be willing to share our blessings with others

Application

Read: Romans 3:23-28

Pray: Thank God for all your many blessings and what He's enabled you to accomplish. Repent of any areas that create an ungodly feeling of pride in your heart.

Reflect: What are some of your greatest accomplishments? How will you share God's blessings to you with others? Do so today.

Day 11 - <u>Whose Ship?</u>

And, behold, there arose a great tempest in the sea, insomuch that the ship was covered with the waves: but he was asleep. And his disciples came to him, and awoke him, saying, Lord, save us: we perish. And he saith unto them, Why are ye fearful, O ye of little faith? Then he arose, and rebuked the winds and the sea; and there was a great calm.
Matthew 8:24-26

My husband's parents have taken many cruises all over the south-Pacific and parts of the Atlantic. We have seen their pictures and enjoyed hearing about their adventures, but we ourselves have never taken a pleasure cruise. We have, however, been on passenger ships to get us from a mainland to an island, like Vancouver to Vancouver Island and I traveled by ship from mainland Nova Scotia to Newfoundland. During this passage the sea was extremely tempest and many people suffered with seasickness. I could certainly understand the above Scripture — even a large ship is no match for the mighty roaring waves of the sea, especially when the waves seem higher than the ship itself. It is easy to be afraid and wonder if you'll cross over without first drowning.

In many ways, ships are a good analogy to our faith. Perhaps this is why there are many songs and hymns written that use this analogy. One time I had a visual picture of faith and ships. I saw myself in a dingy, one that was torn, old and weathered. The weather was tempest, the clouds dark and threatening. All I could see was the disrepair of my dilapidated dingy and the threatening dark clouds, even feel the sensation of sticky wet rain and the wind blowing through my sea-soaked clothes. But then I saw something else — I had a larger view of the dingy and it was actually sitting on the deck of a large ocean-liner, with the Lord Himself as the Captain. This expanded vision started putting

Day 11

things into focus for me and my whole perspective of what I thought was a perilous situation, changed to one of remarkable peace. I realized that there are times in my life when all I see are the storms all around me and the dingy of my own limited resources is inadequate to get me through. I also saw that when unexpected storms arise, I tend to look at the bleak and discouraging circumstances rather than focus on God and His many hope-filled promises.

I believe God allows us to experience the big storms of life because He knows they are no match for our limited resources. In doing so, He hopes we will instead turn to Him and see how great are His resources that are available to us when we simply ask. In the opening verses, we are astounded that Jesus is asleep in the ship with the storm raging all around Him. Why does He seem to take it all so casually and then rebuke His disciples for having such little faith? The disciples had already witnessed great miracles from Jesus and here He was, right with them physically in the boat, and still they were afraid. It is the same with us. Jesus does miraculous things for us every single day (He protects us from harm, He provides for us, He keeps us healthy, etc.), and He is with us in Spirit, yet we fail to recognize Him and remember that He is always with us. May we keep the image of Jesus as our Captain foremost in our minds, especially when life's storms rage all around us, and know that He is always with us guiding us to a safe place.

Application

Read: Matthew 8:23-27

Pray: That God will help you to see Him and believe His promises instead of looking at unfavorable circumstances in your life.

Reflect: When are some times God has brought you through troublesome circumstances? What did you learn? Share this with a troubled soul today.

Day 12 - <u>Dream Source</u>

But the wisdom that is from above is first pure, then peaceable, gentle, and easy to be intreated, full of mercy and good fruits, without partiality, and without hypocrisy. James 3:17

Have you ever known a dreamer? Or maybe you are a dreamer. I'm a dreamer and I know other dreamers. My husband is somewhat of a dreamer, so he and I have had lots of fun creating big dreams that we hope will one day be fulfilled. For one thing, we hope to one day travel throughout the continent and that God will use us as His special messengers to minister to people we meet along the way. On a larger scale, I would like to own and operate a fully-equipped printing and publishing warehouse. With all my heart I want to spread the good news of the Gospel to as many people as possible, and also encourage other Christians in their walk with the Lord. But, I must confess, I have sometimes had other grand dreams that are selfish and self-serving, like winning the lottery with little thought to the good I could do others with that money.

While we need our dreams to look forward to, we also need to discern if our desires/dreams are from God or not. If they are not from God, then we are just chasing after the wind, because it will not be blessed if it does not bless God and others. A sure way to test our source of dreams is if we feel envious towards someone who has something we don't have, so we strive to compete to get it. Or if it causes us to feel discontent and unhappy until we get it, this is not from God. One way to tell if a dream is from God is that if it seems to open other doors and will also bless others. For example, one of my dreams and desires was to learn how to sew. I saw my talented mother sew up many marvellous creations, like elegant dresses for me and my sisters all the while growing up, and I wanted to be able to sew my own clothes when I was a teenager. I did know how to sew by hand, sew buttons and do minor repairs, but I had never learned how to operate a sewing machine. For one reason or another, this desire was not fulfilled until much later, years after I got married. When I got my first sewing machine I was so excited, I stayed up until 5:00 a.m. reading the manual cover to cover and trying different stitches and different settings. Then two years later, a friend gave me a higher-end sewing machine and serger that was no longer being used. Sewing has opened up a whole world of possibilities to me. Since then I have sewed complete outfits, purses, quilts for every size bed, curtains, creative wall-art hangings and more. I have even sold some of my sewing projects and given some away as gifts. I am always experimenting with material and thread and trying something new — in fact, I see it as an art and I thank God for opening this up to me.

On a practical level, when discerning the source of dreams, we need to count the cost and ask ourselves: Can I afford to do this? Do I have time to pursue this? Will it benefit me, others and God in good ways? Will my family life suffer in some way? Will my spiritual life suffer? I like the opening verse to use as a check-list to tell if something (even a thought) is from God or not. May we keep on dreaming big, and all in the hopes it will in some way further God's kingdom and bring great joy to God, others and ourselves.

Application

<u>Read</u>: Ecclesiastes 5

<u>Pray</u>: Ask God to help you discern the source of your dreams, and to remove the ones He has not inspired.

<u>Reflect</u>: What are your dreams? What are you doing to see them fulfilled? Make a plan to fulfill at least one dream.

Day 13 - <u>Overcoming Trials</u>

Therefore being justified by faith, we have peace with God through our Lord Jesus Christ: By whom also we have access by faith into this grace wherein we stand, and rejoice in hope of the glory of God. And not only so, but we glory in tribulations also: knowing that tribulation worketh patience; And patience, experience; and experience, hope: And hope maketh not ashamed; because the love of God is shed abroad in our hearts by the Holy Ghost which is given unto us. Romans 5:1-5

There's a movie where the main character is a TV weatherman and goes to Punxsutawney, PA for the annual Groundhog Day festivities, mainly to see if the groundhog can see his shadow, which determines how long the winter will last. He has a chip on his shoulder thinking he is above this job, treats his boss and co-worker with contempt, and cares little for anyone except himself. They are only supposed to report the festivities, then drive back to the city, but they become stranded when a blizzard hits, so they stay another night. But a strange thing happens the next morning when he gets up — he notices that it's the same day. Everything is the same as the day before, but he's the only one who experiences this. Then the next day the same thing happens and he ends up re-living the same day over and over again. In desperation to escape this strange happening, he tries to kill himself, get himself arrested and even tries to kill the groundhog, but still he wakes up on February 2nd each day.

About three quarters of the way through the movie, he starts to accept his predicament and starts to make some changes with his life. Finally, we see him as a likable, talented and humbled man, which provides the escape from February 2nd to a new day, February 3rd. By this time, he has grown to like the town, and the people whom he only saw

Day 13

as nameless faces, are now his friends and people he cares about. In fact, he decides he wants to stay and live here.

I like this movie for several reasons, but mostly, because you can see how when a person is severely tested, that either they will make the best of things, or turn bitter and fight the lessons that God is trying to teach us. And it is often after we accept our unfavorable circumstances, and decide to make the best of things, that things begin to turn around in our favor. In the case of the main character in this movie, although his circumstances needed changing, he needed to be changed even more. And it is often the same with us. We hope things will change and yet we resist changing our attitude and our way of thinking and living. Or we may expect others to change to suit us, but this is really a way to avoid making our own changes.

In the opening verses, we see that tribulations produce patience and patience teaches us and strengthens us, which gives us hope and therefore enables us to endure and even triumph over future trials when they come. As Christians, we can trust God to bring us through from one mundane and difficult day to a new and blessed one, because we know He is actively changing us through our difficult circumstances and has promised to see us through them all.

Application

<u>Read</u>: 1 Peter 1:3-9

<u>Pray</u>: Ask God to reveal any areas where change is needed. Ask Him to help you accept your circumstances no matter how difficult.

<u>Reflect</u>: Have you ever felt a need to escape an unpleasant situation? What happened? What did you learn from it?

Day 14 - <u>Blurred Vision</u>

And Jesus answered and said unto him, What wilt thou that I should do unto thee? The blind man said unto him, Lord, that I might receive my sight. And Jesus said unto him, Go thy way; thy faith hath made thee whole. And immediately he received his sight, and followed Jesus in the way. Mark 10:51-52

Almost every year I go to the optometrist to get my eyes checked. This is necessary since there was blindness on my father's side of the family. Usually I have routine tests, since my vision is good and I don't have to wear corrective lenses (except for reading small print). The last time I went, the optometrist said she wanted to give me an extra test, called a "dilation" test. In this test she could see the muscles behind my eyes to determine if they were healthy and normal. After she explained that I would need someone to come with me so they could drive me home, I felt apprehensive and wanted to know more about the test. She said that my pupils would abnormally dilate and everything would become brighter like on a bright sunny day.

The morning that I had the test, while the drops stung momentarily, the strangest thing did happen — I felt as if my vision was actually widening, and also that I was wearing a very greasy pair of glasses. Everything became distorted and when I went to write the check to pay for the exam, I couldn't see properly, so my husband had to write it instead. Since it was sunny outside, I put on a pair of sunglasses, but still the strange blurriness persisted. I couldn't judge distances, so of course, I couldn't drive. It seemed that everything was brighter and nothing focused properly. It remained like this for a few hours.

While I was experiencing this blurred fog, and it was difficult to even walk correctly, I started to realize how blessed I was to have such good vision. I felt so thankful and

Day 14

grateful to God for giving me such a priceless gift. I also realized how I had taken my vision for granted and that I had taken so many other gifts of God for granted as well. Then I saw a spiritual application — when we take things for granted, this in itself is a form of blurred vision, because we fail to see the goodness of God in granting us so many blessings in the first place. And it is often not until we lose something we have taken for granted that we realize what a blessing it is or has been, and how gracious God is to us.

There is another lesson in this too. In the opening verses, blind Bartimaeus was so incapacitated with his lack of sight that he resorted to begging for his food. But when he heard that Jesus was coming his way, he got so excited that others tried to quiet him down. He begged Jesus for mercy and that he would heal his eyes that he might see again. And Jesus healed him based on the faith he had. This is a great story because blind Bartimaeus had only "heard" about Jesus and still he believed that Jesus would heal him. Many had physically seen miracles of Jesus and still, did not believe in Him. Bartimaeus may have been blind physically, but he had sight when it came to spiritual things; he had the faith to believe even when he couldn't see. This is the sight that really counts. Our physical sight shows us many things, yet can't provide the faith we need when we really need it. May we look instead for the real vision, which is spiritual, and look to Jesus to guide us to the true path of life and peace.

Application

Read: Mark 10:46-52

Pray: Thank God for your many blessings and ask Him to reveal any weak areas where you might have blurred vision.

Reflect: What are some things you have taken for granted? Make a list and then thank God for each and every one. Share God's goodness with someone today.

Day 15 - <u>Making Resolutions</u>

Brethren, I count not myself to have apprehended: but this one thing I do, forgetting those things which are behind, and reaching forth unto those things which are before, Philippians 3:13

Have you ever gone to a New Year's celebration excited about the New Year ahead and yet experienced some nagging regrets about the year that is ending because you didn't accomplish all that you had hoped? I sure have. Every year for several years I'd make a new list of New Year's resolutions and then try to follow them, so that I could feel as if I was accomplishing some worthy goals in my life. One of my resolutions was to lose weight. This was followed closely by, "get into shape." Then I might add, "to get out of debt." In better financial years I'd write, "buy a new car, or take a trip to Disneyland or the Grand Canyon." Many times I'd start to succeed, like when I'd start on a diet, but then a few months later, I would have gained it all back again. New Year's resolutions can be good if they keep us on track and provide inspiration to try new things, but they can also be a means to discourage us if we'd made the wrong resolutions, or if we continue to fail at completing them.

One year one of my resolutions did come true — I wanted to get married and find the right husband, but God found Him for me and we've been living happily ever after ever since. But come to think of it, I did little to bring this about, other than be willing to allow God to prepare me for this huge and rewarding life step. Many of our resolutions can't be completed without God's help and intervention. And I believe that this is the way God planned it, so we would turn to Him and develop a personal and meaningful relationship with Him based on love, trust and obedience to His perfect guidance in our lives. Also, sometimes my resolutions far exceed what I am even able to accomplish, both physically and financially, and I have to abandon them altogether. This once happened when I had booked a flight to London, England. The closer the time came to travel, the more nervous I became because I was traveling alone and didn't want to go without a traveling companion, so I canceled my trip. As I've grown and matured, I have changed my perspective on making New Years resolutions because I believe it is better to take one prayerful day at a time and allow God to unfold His perfect will rather than settle for my own lofty impossible-to-attain imperfect goals.

Also, in some cases, my New Years resolutions have carried over for so many years, they have been more of a weight and a burden than something to look forward to achieving. So, like Paul, I have left them behind, "forgetting those things which are behind" and moved forward "reaching forth unto those things" newly set before me. Nothing is set in stone and this makes the Christian life so rewarding and exciting. I think God likes to surprise us and fulfill our heart's desire in a time we least expect it. This way He gets the praise and honor and glory. But if it's me achieving my own goals and keeping on schedule like clock-work, then I can take personal credit for it and the praise might go to me instead of God. May we always make sure when and if we are going to make New Years resolutions or set goals, that they are prayerfully made and we take God's hand and draw on His strength and power to fulfill them.

Application

Read: Philippians 3:3-14

Pray: Go over your New Years resolutions and/or goals with God at the start of each year. Continue to seek His guidance and strength throughout the year.

Reflect: What are some of your New Years resolutions and/or goals? Describe your successes and your failures. What new resolutions will you make that glorify God and help others?

Day 16 - <u>Gardening in All Seasons</u>

He that observeth the wind shall not sow; and he that regardeth the clouds shall not reap.
Ecclesiastes 11:4

One cloudy and windy day late in May, I decided to go outside and start weeding one of my flower beds close to the house in the back yard. The weather had been cloudy and rainy for several days, so was not ideal for gardening or other outdoor activities. But since I was struggling with depression from experiencing so much gloominess and intermittent rain, I decided to do my gardening anyway. I am sure anyone seeing me out in the rain that was spitting off and on might have wondered about me, but I was determined to make a difference in at least one of my flower beds.

While I was plucking and firmly pulling at the weeds and long prairie grass that had infested this 4 x 5 foot flower bed, I noticed that I not only started feeling better, but my flower bed was starting to show it's true colors — what all gardeners love to see — fresh black dirt where once unsightly weeds and grass had grown. Another good thing is that whenever I work in the garden, I seem to feel much closer to the Lord, the One who created the first and most beautiful garden, The Garden of Eden. As I was struggling with depression, I felt the Lord say, "No matter how bad things seem I will always be with you, helping you pull out and root out the bad weeds of your life." I knew immediately that the bad weeds for me were the negative thoughts that were dragging me down emotionally.

Like our gardens, sometimes our lives become infested with weeds, sometimes beyond our control and sometimes due to our own neglect. When things pile up, the garden of our life will look terrible at first and the thought of cleaning it up will seem so overwhelming that we will want to run away after just one glance. And it is easy to put things off, like I

Day 16

might have done in real gardening and just wait until the weather improved. But if we wait for ideal conditions, sometimes they won't come at all, and then we get even further behind. Our problems can be like that, too. They pile up because we don't want to deal with them. When gardening, I noticed that the cleaner my garden was getting, the better I started to feel. Not only was I accomplishing something that needed to get done, but because I was so focused on the task, my negative thoughts melted away and I felt emotionally uplifted.

Another lesson is that I started to see the flower garden as the growing-field of my mind. I need to pull out the negative roots of my thinking and sometimes ruthlessly yank out stubborn and persistently negative thoughts. And I need to spot new negative small thoughts (like fear and worry) and pull them out before they grow any bigger. Fear never gets smaller — it only increases the more we feed it. I need to be careful not to give any ground in my mind for fear, for it will surely take over and choke out the good thoughts that are there. Once the negative thoughts are pulled out, we see a dark, black field of soil. Now it is time to plant something that will yield a good crop — it may be beautiful and fragrant thoughts that are praiseworthy and bless others, or it may be vegetables from God's Word that sustains us. So we must work toward the pure black soil of healthy thinking no matter how inclement the weather.

Application

<u>Read</u>: Hebrews 4:12-16

<u>Pray</u>: Ask God to help you clean up your mind and rid you of any thoughts that are not from Him.

<u>Reflect</u>: Do you have any thoughts that need to be weeded out? Think about what new and healthy thoughts you will plant there instead.

Day 17 - <u>A Comforting Psalm</u>

He maketh me to lie down in green pastures: he leadeth me beside the still waters. He restoreth my soul: Psalm 23:2-3a

One of my favorite Psalms is Psalm 23. This is one of the Psalms that we really need to take time to read and meditate on, because I believe that when we really apply it and take it to heart, it will greatly reduce stress in our lives. It also has a calming effect, and can still the fear in our thoughts and minds.

This was brought home to me when I sat at the bedside of my mother-in-law who was dying of cancer. It was the first Scripture that I read to her and seemed fitting to bring her peace and comfort in her last hours on this earth. She had been battling cancer for 17 years and had taken every kind of medication and treatment available, but still, the cancer persisted. My husband and I, family and friends had been praying for her for a full year for her healing and also that she would be drawn much closer to the Lord through all the fear and uncertainty that she was facing.

When we suffer with illness, and especially for people diagnosed with cancer, fear is the first thing to strike people's hearts because often it means that a person not only has a long and difficult battle ahead, but may also not win that battle and instead succumb to an untimely death. This is why Scriptures such as Psalm 23 are so powerful and reassuring when the doctors have done all they can and the final outcome is in God's hands.

My mother-in-law had lived a full life, raising four wonderful boys and enjoying six healthy grandchildren. She loved knitting and sewing and making beautiful sweaters and scarves for each of us. She loved traveling and took many Caribbean cruises after my father-in-law retired from the railway. We all loved her and were greatly saddened when we

Day 17

heard of the news of the cancer returning. In the last couple weeks, we believe she knew she was dying and did not want to be alone. So we visited her and prayed with her because we knew that only Jesus could remove her fear. When we were called the morning she was rushed into the hospital, we came to say goodbye knowing that the Lord was with her, that she was in His hands and that He'd take care of her.

When people are not spiritually prepared to die, they will be agitated, afraid and ornery. They will not always be open to hear the Gospel, or "good news" even at the point of death, when it is their last chance to accept God's free gift of salvation. But my mother-in-law was at peace. She willingly listened as we read her Scripture, sang to her and continued to pray with her. At the time of her passing, my husband said, "It's time to go now. Don't be afraid. Jesus is coming for you." And a little while later, I had a vision of her walking through a wide door. She was young again and Jesus stood there and took her hand. It was a precious scene and one I will never forget. When all is said and done, only the Lord can give remarkable peace in the midst of what life tries to rob us of — only Jesus can lead us beside still waters and restore our souls. He'll do this for us throughout our life, and even in death, there is nothing to fear, but a quiet peace that He is with us.

Application

Read: Psalm 23

Pray: Whatever you may be struggling with in your life, turn everything over to the Lord and ask Him to comfort you.

Reflect: Take time to read Psalm 23. Meditate on it and picture Jesus with you. Journal what happens when you do this. Share Psalm 23 with someone in need today.

Day 18 - <u>Getting Good News</u>

Many have undertaken to draw up an account of the things that have been fulfilled among us, just as they were handed down to us by those who from the first were eyewitnesses and servants of the word. Therefore, since I myself have carefully investigated everything from the beginning, it seemed good also to me to write an orderly account for you, most excellent Theophilus, so that you may know the certainty of the things you have been taught.
Luke 1:1-4 NIV

Years ago I used to write letters to friends I had met at summer Bible camp or friends from other churches who lived far away. I had one pen pal from Saskatchewan that I wrote to regularly until we were well into our 20s. I always looked forward to hearing from her. I still write short letters and send out cards, although most of my correspondence is via email. Also, it seems easier and faster to phone someone rather than sit down and write letters like I used to.

Communication has always been important. In the old days, people corresponded by mail or news traveled by word of mouth. Sometimes the mail would take weeks or even months to reach someone depending on the distance and the difficulty of reaching a community due to weather or difficult trails since there wouldn't have been paved roads or even automobiles invented yet.

Even thousands of years ago, communication was very important. In the opening passage of Scripture, the writer Luke is about to give the important account of how the birth of John the Baptist came about, and how it was a prelude to the long-awaited coming of the Lord Jesus Christ. These were exciting times indeed and through the birth of John and later Jesus, the beginning of an evangelistic mission began that would one day reach the whole world, known as the Gospel or the "good news." Truly it was and is the most important

Day 18

message ever proclaimed to mankind.

In New Testament Biblical times, important news was delivered by letter and also word of mouth. I marvel at the accuracy of the words written by men who were inspired by God. This Good News of the coming of the Lord Jesus Christ was broadcast far and wide and many people looked forward to this incredible event. People today do not realize the magnitude of the importance of the coming of the Lord. For the Jewish nation, it meant the fulfillment of prophecies found in Genesis and also in Isaiah and in many other Scriptures throughout the Old Testament. This good news and coming of the Lord had been told for generations over hundreds, even thousands of years. It meant a new freedom from bondage to sin, sickness, slavery, and ultimately death, or eternal separation from God. Jesus was the promised Messiah, a great Deliverer coming to set His people free, and also for all who believe in Him, including Gentiles and every person born into this world for all time. It was indeed a huge and significant event — none would ever be as far-reaching or life-changing. Still today, each and every follower and believer of Jesus Christ (Who died and rose again and saved us from our sin), carry this "good news" of the Gospel message. There is no greater message and may we faithfully, like Luke did for Theophilus, share this good news and keep it uppermost, using every form of communication we have available to us today.

Application

<u>Read</u>: Luke 1:26-38

<u>Pray</u>: Pray for every opportunity to share the good news of the Gospel message to all who need to hear it.

<u>Reflect</u>: What is some good news you have received in your lifetime? Write about it. Tell someone how you heard about the Gospel message and invite them to receive salvation.

Day 19 - <u>Hand-Me Downs</u>

But continue thou in the things which thou hast learned and hast been assured of, knowing of whom thou hast learned them; 2 Timothy 3:14

In the days of old (and still in some cases today), people who had big families often couldn't afford to buy new clothes for each of their children. It was enough to try and keep food on the table and pay other necessary bills just to survive. So clothes would be handed down from the oldest to the youngest as each child started to outgrow his or her clothes. These clothes were known as "hand-me downs."

But there are other hand-me downs, other than clothes, that might be considered priceless and that have great sentimental value. For instance, when a grandparent passes away, a wedding ring might be handed down to a daughter, which is then passed down to a granddaughter. A pocket watch might be handed down to a son or a grandson. And still, there are more practical hand-me downs like favorite family recipes. My grandmother on my mother's side was Austrian and was an expert cook making every kind of Slavic dish imaginable. So in our home, perogies, cabbage rolls, and borsch were often served.

But there is another hand-me down, or rather "legacy," that was passed down to me from my mother's parents and that is, the legacy of faith. When I was researching her extensive family history, I wanted her story and that of each of her siblings. My grandmother had 21 children. All the while I was growing up I knew 15 of the ones that were left. I ended up with 17 stories not including my grandparents, who had already passed away. One of the main purposes of writing the history was to know how they each had become Christians, since I had felt that their impact on society and even on the world was significant since ministers, missionaries, evangelists and pastors came out of this family. As I read their stories, I noticed similarities in beliefs, in how they were converted and in what they had done with their lives. In almost every testimony, their conversion to Christianity was miraculous and life-changing, as mine also was. They felt called into ministry, as I also do. They made spreading the Gospel a priority, as I was also taught to do. This is not a coincidence, since they each left home and went their separate ways. This was a result of my grandparent's diligent prayers that followed their children and grand-children and now great-grandchildren for generations to come.

Shortly after I had returned home from Bible school where my life had been changed, I read the opening verse and the one following it. It had great personal significance for me because my relatives also believed the same and supported me in my faith. My parents had taught me about God and had schooled me in the Bible from the time I was born. Through the years, I knew friends who had not come from a Christian background, and they'd remark how blessed I was to have been given such a tremendous legacy. For parents today, who perhaps don't even attend church, the greatest hand-me down you can give your children is the legacy of faith. This is the one that truly counts and this is the only one they'll ever need.

Application

Read: 2 Timothy 3:14-17

Pray: Pray for God to show you how you can pass on a legacy of faith to your children and to others. If necessary, pray for your own family to be saved.

Reflect: What has been handed down to you? What will you hand down to your children and/or others? Consider how you will hand down a legacy of faith.

Day 20 - <u>Mount St. Helens</u>

But the day of the Lord will come as a thief in the night; in the which the heavens shall pass away with a great noise, and the elements shall melt with fervent heat, the earth also and the works that are therein shall be burned up. 2 Peter 3:10

I remember the day Mount St. Helens erupted (May 18, 1980). It was all over the news and on every TV station. It was a catastrophic event caused by an earthquake that measured 5.1 on the Richter scale. A large portion of the north side of the mountain collapsed causing a massive rock debris avalanche that rippled over 230 square miles of forestry destroying and burying everything in its fierce destructive path. As well, molten ash erupted from deep inside of the mountain, shooting thousands of feet upward and then drifted downward turning normal daylight into a strange darkness. For nine hours the mountain erupted.

Even as far away as Winnipeg (from Washington) which is about 1,645 miles, I noticed the grayness of the day and a few days after that. It was hard to believe that this eruption would move across the country so quickly and affect every living thing so noticeably. For instance, I remember going outside to my car and finding a layer of fine ash covering it. In fact, everything was covered — vehicles, houses, windows and trees. Even the sky was gray, although you knew that the sun was behind the grayness because the temperature was warm. The air quality was affected and at times it was hard to breathe. It was strange and eerie being affected by an event that seemed so far removed.

The eruption of Mount St. Helens went down in history as the deadliest and most economically disruptive volcano in US history, killing 57 people, destroying 250 homes and many miles of bridges, rail lines, highways and nearby forestry. Yet this is only one isolated event in only one

Day 20

corner of the world. When we read prophetic Scripture from the Bible, we can't even imagine what awaits our natural world even though people will try everything to save the environment and this tiny planet that we all live on. We may read the opening passage of Scripture and think that this sounds unreal, something we can't relate to, something that will never happen in our lifetime. So we pass it off and lay it aside, thinking it will never apply to us in a real or tangible way.

While we may never live to experience "the day of the Lord" in our lifetime, still the Bible has left us signs and warnings that we must not ignore. We emphasize the love and grace of God in our lives, but we must also revere and respect the Lord as a righteous judge who will come and bring to submission every living and created thing that He created for His pleasure and glory. We think of Him in awe at His ability to subdue all things for His own purposes, mainly to point us to the mighty works of God and to bring people to Him for the salvation of their souls. Even just experiencing one catastrophic event such as the eruption of Mount St. Helens is enough to create a kind of awe at the power of nature that God created and uses to show us His magnificence. We must never take lightly the awesome power of God, but always be ready for the day of the Lord, whether it's in our lifetime or not.

Application

<u>Read</u>: 2 Peter 3:10-14

<u>Pray</u>: Pray that you and others will always be ready for the return of the Lord. Pray for those who you know are not ready to meet the Lord.

<u>Reflect</u>: Has any catastrophic event ever affected your life? If so, write about it. What will you do to prepare for the day of the Lord?

Day 21 - <u>Being Stedfast</u>

Therefore, my beloved brethren, be ye stedfast, unmoveable, always abounding in the work of the Lord, forasmuch as ye know that your labour is not in vain in the Lord. 1 Corinthians 15:58

One mild winter on a Saturday afternoon, my husband and I attended a local community hockey game in the city. Our 10 year old nephew was playing on the "White" team (according to their hockey outfits which were white) against the "Black" team who were wearing black hockey outfits. We were sitting next to the parents of the black team, and some of the fathers were yelling as loud as they could to their boys to cheer them on. But we couldn't help but notice how quiet the cheering was for the white team. In fact, I felt that the parents of the black team were actually distracting the boys on the white team and interfering with their performance. When I mentioned this to my husband, he started yelling even louder to cheer on the white team.

This reminds me of the times we may be trying to do good and something happens to discourage us. Maybe we've just given more than our share of tithe to the church and then the next thing you know, we receive an unexpected bill that we can hardly afford to pay. Or maybe everything has been going well physically with our bodies, and then we receive an upsetting test result from the doctor and we find out that our health is at risk. Any number of things can happen in a single day to take our minds off of doing good and doing the Lord's work, and instead cause us to re-focus on the problems that we are presented with.

For example, for many years I wanted to write an in-depth book on backsliding from a Biblical viewpoint, based on my own experience with backsliding. But it took me many years to actually sit down and write it through, and several more years to re-write it and get it to a place where it was

Day 21

ready to publish. All the while my good intentions were there, the distractions to actually finish the work were too numerous to count. Something always came up that seemed to compete for my immediate attention and the backsliding book would be shelved time and time again.

Finally, God allowed certain circumstances to occur that would not only give me time to complete it, but to also publish it myself. With no vehicle, this would mean that I would be unable to continue my part-time job outside of the home. It was winter and I wouldn't be going out much since I would be snowed in. And since we were living in a rural area, there really wasn't too much in the way of social activity to distract me away. So finally, I was able to completely finish and publish the book. Many times I wondered why God had me in such a tight place, where He had intervened and narrowed my many choices of things I could do to only one (to write and publish the book). But soon I came to realize that with all the distractions gone, that God wanted to speak to me and teach me many valuable lessons about Himself. He also wanted to teach me to trust Him even though I couldn't see the final results or understand why it was so important to finish this book. Throughout our life, we will be presented with choices — to turn to the things of this world and allow the busyness of life that surrounds us to distract us, or we will choose to be stedfast ... **always abounding in the work of the Lord.**

Application

<u>Read</u>: Luke 9:23-26

<u>Pray</u>: **for God to help you be able to discern what you should be doing and what you should avoid doing. Do this daily.**

<u>Reflect</u>: **Other than your work, what do you spend your time doing? Re-focus where needed and make a new schedule where you include more spiritual things you can do for the Lord.**

Day 22 – <u>Survival Guide</u>

And all things, whatsoever ye shall ask in prayer, believing, ye shall receive. Matthew 21:22

An elderly woman from our area was going to visit her brother when she got stranded in the winter on a country road. She had no food or cell phone, but she did have a meager survival kit in her car which contained some matches, a candle, a scarf, leg warmers and men's woolen socks. For four days no one drove by or noticed her. But she determined to survive rather than feel sorry for herself and give up. At first, she tried to summon help by opening the trunk to attract passers by, then she attached a red mitten to the radio antenna, and she also left her flashers on all night, but still no one noticed her. The second day her car battery died. In the next two days that followed she tried other things to attract attention — she built a fire out of a catalogue, and another time burned a cardboard box she found in the car. Still no help arrived. In the meantime she found a plastic container and using her now depleting match supply, melted snow which turned into water, and she drank that. She also found an antacid which was her only nourishment. On the morning of the fifth day, a local farmer passed by and rescued her. She was fine and had survived her long ordeal of trying to survive in the winter on a stranded country road by using her wits and also through prayer.

A few years ago a similar thing happened to a young woman traveling at night on her way from the city to our area up north and she got lost. But she did have a cell phone. The only problem was, she didn't know where she was since it was dark and it was blizzard conditions and there was no way to trace her call. But a search party did finally find her once she explained the roads she had taken thus far. Still, it was a miracle they found her at all.

Day 22

I was stranded on the highway in the winter twice while traveling to and from my hometown to the city where I lived and worked. I was alone both times and both times it was a holiday. The first time it was Christmas Eve day and I lost power since the distributor cap was iced up. A nice family followed me to a nearby city close to my hometown and I left the car at the garage where my parents picked me up and drove me the rest of the way. The second time it was night and I also lost power as I did the first time. But this time I prayed and miraculously regained speed and made it home over 100 miles to the city.

Authorities tell us that if we are ever stranded in the winter to never walk away from the vehicle, but stay inside away from cold winter winds that can freeze skin in a matter of minutes. They also advise to always carry an emergency kit with items that will carry us through for days at a time. But I believe that the greatest survival tool we have is prayer. In the opening verse we have one of the most amazing promises in the whole Bible — God will grant us "all things" we ask of Him and also if we believe. While it is good and wise to carry material survival kits when traveling, and also to use caution and our wits when we do travel in inclement weather, we must always keep in mind that some things can and will happen beyond our control. Praying to God with confidence will see us through any situation.

Application

Read: Proverbs 3:1-8

Pray: Ask God for whatever your needs may be, and believe He loves you, is with you and will answer you.

Reflect: Think about the times God has pulled you through difficult situations. Why is prayer the greatest survival guide we have? Journal your thoughts.

Day 23 - <u>Color Your World</u>

Now faith is the substance of things hoped for, the evidence of things not seen. Hebrews 11:1

The first time I really experimented with color for decorating a home was after we bought a spacious condo that had a few hundred square feet of walls to paint. The walls were all pale pastel and white and all blended into one bland scheme, or so I thought. So I picked up a paint brochure with several color swatches and started picking out colors for each room. I started with the bedroom. I picked a warm tan tone contrasted with a deep china blue tone. Being used to the pastels, I was fine with the tan color, but aghast when I saw the deepness of the blue color. Losing sleep the first night was just the beginning of my "color jitters" as each time I tried a somewhat bold but classic color, and felt the insecurity and "painters remorse" of the color now firmly affixed to the once placid wall.

Being an artist I had studied the values and hues of color, but with windows in three different directions, walls that were anything but conventionally situated, and a color scheme already begun by bright woodsy cork flooring, darker laminate flooring and white ceramic kitchen tiles, not to mention pale green and gold fleck counters in the kitchen and main bathroom, my color choices were numerous and daunting. I had to take into consideration all of these factors and then decide on a color scheme for the entire two floor condo (including stairways and hallways). But I had prayed about my color choices and felt that the chosen colors were definitely inspired in spite of my angst once I saw them on the walls. For one thing I was seeing them with blind faith — most of the laminate flooring had not been put in yet, and there was no furniture, so I had nothing to gage the color against.

Being troubled, I prayed and asked the Lord if I had

mistakenly picked these colors even though I believe He had guided me in the choices. I received an immediate interesting answer — that once the furniture was in, wall hangings were hung and lighting was in place, the colors would all harmonize and everything would look really good. Then a spiritual application came to mind. Many times when we see a problem (or perceive it to be one), we immediately panic and assume the worst. We do this even though many things will and do happen beyond our control that will pull the situation together and work out for the ultimate good in the end. God wants us to look to Him for everything, when things are good and when things seem to be going wrong. He wants to get the glory and show us the way He works — which is more often than not, miraculous.

There was another lesson as well — even though my color choices may not be the latest and greatest and in some cases follow no "color" chart at all, as a Christian I am also called to be different and not follow the fads and fashion whims of the world. Even though I may be tempted to do what others do or try to fit in, God wants me to just be myself even if my color scheme doesn't match the same standards of the professionals. As my condo is a work in progress, so am I and I look forward to see what God unfolds in my life one colorful situation at a time.

Application

Read: Hebrews 11:1-6

Pray: for understanding regarding any difficult situation you are in. Ask God to help you see a positive outcome.

Reflect: What do you struggle with that causes you great anxiety? Write about things God brought you through and what you learned from it. Share it with someone.

Day 24 - <u>Serving or Solicitation?</u>

For, brethren, ye have been called unto liberty; only use not liberty for an occasion to the flesh, but by love serve one another. **Galatians 5:13**

Have you ever heard an advertisement where a company says, "We're here to serve you better?" Or they say, "Serving [your area] for the past 10 years." In some ways this is a pretence of what true servanthood means. It is a misuse of the term "to serve," because rather than serve for selfless reasons, it is really a way to get people to shop at a certain place and continue to shop there. Companies are trying to make money and will do almost anything to build a customer base and get as much of the marketing share as possible. In other words, in marketing, to serve is just another way of saying, "I'll serve you, but for a price." It is an exchange of service for money.

Not that there is anything wrong with offering services when we buy something, but we must never confuse the kind of service marketing offers with the kind of service Jesus exemplified and taught. I'd like to illustrate how true servanthood was demonstrated to me and my husband after we moved into a condominium in the city. My sister and her husband, who lead full and busy lives, offered to help us move. They took time to help us move things from our house over an hour away from our condo, and about an hour from their home on the outskirts of the city. Then my sister ran to my rescue after I had agonized over what color to paint the many walls throughout the spacious condo. She went out of her way from a busy day at work and more busyness awaiting her at home, to help me make choices to calm my living area color scheme and pull all the colors together. This meant a great deal to me since I found it very stressful. She has come to my rescue countless other times when it has been a sacrifice of time and resources for her.

Day 24

Another friend showed us true servanthood one day when my husband had to take our car into the garage, about 20 minutes from where we live. She was at the garage also and offered to give my husband a ride home to save him from taking the bus (which would have taken about two hours) or a taxi. Then two days later she came and picked us up to take us back to the garage to pick up our vehicle. In both cases, my sister and my friend asked for nothing in return, but followed the opening verse, "by love serve one another." I know that this is the lifestyle they lead as I hear of others who have been blessed by these two angels.

There is something tangible about this kind of love — you see it, you experience it and you benefit by it. You see God's love at work first hand. This is a powerful testimony of God's love. In fact, when we contrast the two types of serving, there is a marked difference that shows that there are really two completely opposite systems in place — the world system that is looking to get something, and the Kingdom of God, that is looking to give something. May we always strive to further the Kingdom of God, be willing to freely give of ourselves and not get confused by the world system and think that true service is an exchange of give and take.

Application

Read: 1 Corinthians 9:19-23

Pray: for all those who selflessly serve others daily. Ask God to help you do the same.

Reflect: What have others done for you to selflessly serve you? How will you do the same for others? Ask God to impress someone on your heart that you can serve today; then do whatever you can to be a blessing to that person.

Day 25 - Simplicity

But I fear, lest by any means, as the serpent beguiled Eve through his subtilty, so your minds should be corrupted from the simplicity that is in Christ. 2 Corinthians 11:3

When I was in my late 20s, I enrolled in university in the Arts program with a major in English and minor in Political Studies. Over the next six years (while working full time and taking night courses), I was to receive a full menu of worldly philosophies, all intended to open my mind and teach me academic skills in research writing, and especially critical thinking. The term "critical thinking" means that rather than just take one view of things, you research many other authors and academic professionals and then try to come up with some conclusions about a certain topic or subject. For instance, if I was writing a paper about Hamlet, I would read several journal articles specific to Shakespeare's Hamlet, maybe some books dedicated to the play, go through each of them and discover the main themes of Hamlet.

After six years of being immersed in critical thinking, I came away filled with knowledge and a much broader perspective on the world and especially literature. But I noticed that my spiritual thinking had been adversely affected. When I went to read the Bible, it was like reading a foreign language — it didn't make sense like it used to. This greatly alarmed me. Had I been brainwashed by the liberal ideologies and worldly anti-Christ philosophies of the educational system? I believe that I was. It took at least two years of intensive Bible reading, Christian book reading and prayer for me to be de-programmed so that I would know the truths and power of God's Word once again in my life. In fact, the Word of God had to become a priority in order for me to understand God's thoughts and ways for me.

One of the most dangerous things about critical thinking

Day 25

is that it causes you to doubt. There is nothing wrong in itself in asking questions, for this is how we learn. But it becomes dangerous when we start to question what is true and right according to God's Word. Liberal thinkers would say that this is narrow-minded thinking and fundamentalism. If you think about it, the first original sin occurred with a question that Satan posed to Eve — "***Did God really say, 'You must not eat from any tree in the garden?'***" (Genesis 3:1 NIV). This potent question created doubt which undermined her faith which resulted in disobeying God. In the opening verse, the word "corrupted" is used. Knowledge outside of God's Word that in any way contradicts with the truth is not from God and it must be rejected.

There is a wonderful simplicity in knowing Christ that in no way undermines our use of intelligence. It is a simplicity that is so profound we can't even imagine the depth of it all, because God is eternal. Simplicity is necessary as followers of Christ because without it we can't walk by faith. I believe God created us all with the capacity for greatness and to do great things with our life. But to abuse knowledge or seek it for selfish gain will most often get in the way of us doing great things with our lives that glorify God. May we seek simplicity in our thinking, which is the most profound knowledge of all because it comes from God.

Application

<u>Read</u>: 1 Corinthians 1:18-31

<u>Pray</u>: Ask God to reveal any areas in your life where you have substituted the wisdom of the world for the profound simplicity that is only found in Christ. Pray for restitution.

<u>Reflect</u>: Do you struggle with your thinking in ways that create doubt about God's Word? List them and then turn them over to God. Fill your mind with God's thoughts instead.

Day 26 - <u>The Challenger</u>

And God said, Let us make man in our image, after our likeness: and let them have dominion over the fish of the sea, and over the fowl of the air, and over the cattle, and over all the earth, and over every creeping thing that creepeth upon the earth. Genesis 1:26

I remember the morning of January 28, 1986. I was working as a data entry clerk at a university in Manitoba with a co-worker and supervisor. We were listening to the radio as a big event was taking place — the launching of NASA's Challenger. It was a unique space launch because there was a civilian aboard, Christa McAuliffe, a civilian teacher who was going to broadcast the findings of the mission to school children around the world. But the most unthinkable thing happened during the take-off phase — the Challenger exploded killing all seven people aboard. I remember watching it on the news later, seeing the billowing white streak soar and curve high up into the blue sky and the shrieks of the people down below watching it happen, powerless to intervene. It rocked the world over, since it was the first time a civilian had attempted such a flight.

I remember discussing it with family and friends later and the thought came to us that perhaps NASA was jumping too far ahead in its ambitious plans to allow civilians to go up into space. We thought that perhaps once ordinary men and women become part of the space research programs, we've gone beyond what God had ever intended for us. This is not to say that space research goes against Scripture, but it does not say in the Bible that we are given dominion over the air or space. I've often thought that the billions of dollars spent in the space programs could be far better spent to feed starving people in every country, to help developing countries, pay off huge national debts, or go into medical research. I've also thought that if we consider the mess of things we've made on this earth with respect to environment

Day 26

(such as the global warming issue), wars, self-imposed disease and more, would we not also mismanage other planets? Also, I believe that one of the main purposes for the heavens and the universe is to cause us to look up and behold the unreachable vastness and magnificent power of God — how He holds all the planets in place, how it is mostly unreachable to human hands or even understanding.

If we look back to the beginning of the space program in 1958, or space race, as it came to be called, it all began as a race between nations (the US and Russia) to show who had the biggest and best space program. It was really a competition begun during the Cold War years, a ploy for one Superpower to show up the other. With every new launch, there is a media blitz of the power of man's ability to reach such heights and make discoveries that will in no way save us from the trouble we are already in.

While we may admire man's ability to explore space and even benefit in some ways from Satellite usage and research, ultimately the heavens and beyond are in the domain of the Lord. Some day I believe we will see it all, but rather than draw attention to man and his ability, we will stare in awe at the majesty and power of our amazing and awesome God — the true Creator of all.

Application

Read: Psalm 8:3-9

Pray: that we become responsible for what God's given us dominion over on this earth.

Reflect: What is your opinion regarding space research? Does it line up with Scripture? In what ways could we better improve upon our earth?

Day 27 - <u>A Furry Alarm Clock</u>

Therefore let us not sleep, as do others; but let us watch and be sober. 1 Thessalonians 5:6

Almost every morning, quite early for us, especially on weekends, we hear a BANG BANG BANG on our bedroom door. When we go to open it our two black kittens come scurrying in. Latte runs under the bed where he does calisthenics hanging upside down from the mattress running along underneath from beginning to end. Espresso takes a flying leap over me and lands close to my neck, flops himself down and purrs for about three seconds before he goes to see what mischief his brother has gotten himself into. Needless to say, we rarely get a good long sleep through the night and get to sleep-in in the morning!

They keep us alert in other ways, too. We have a railing on the second and third floor that separates the floors from the stairways. Latte soon discovered them and we've found him precariously trying to walk along the three inch ledge looking down, swaying this way and that almost falling a few times. And Espresso will explore almost anything. If there's an open bag filled with things, he'll dive right in and we'll have to pull him out before he gets lost in it. He also likes to jump into boxes, whatever the size and if there's room, he'll chase his tail and go around in circles a few quick times. They'll eat almost anything, including little pieces of sticky paper and even leftover pieces of rug when we pulled the rugs out to put in laminate flooring. Latte will go into my purse and if he finds a candy with a wrapping, he'll take it out and carry it between his teeth, then run as fast and as far away as he can so we can't catch him and take away his prized candy. Our cats are entertaining and they also teach us many lessons.

For one thing, we need to be alert in our spiritual lives as well. Many times throughout the day I believe the Lord tries

Day 27

to protect us from impending harm. We may find this true after we have read our daily devotions. A situation may come up that alarms or disturbs us and we will remember the verses we read earlier in the day. Maybe we are over-tired and start bickering with a family member or friend. Maybe someone says something to us that makes us feel hurt or angry. Maybe we have worrisome thoughts about our job, money or our loved ones. These are the kinds of thoughts that will steal away the peace that Jesus promised us (see John 14:27).

The Lord will always do His part in keeping us from harm and He will always be there to guide and protect us. But we need to do our part too — avoid potentially harmful situations, and also discern our thought life and not allow negative and ungodly thoughts to stay there and steal away our peace. When we are tired we will be tempted to give in to the flesh and then Satan has a hey-day with us. But if we read the Word and continue in prayer, we will do as the above verse says, "watch and be sober." We need to have our wits about us. With the knowledge of God and His truth, we are responsible to live accordingly as He continues to reveal more and more of His ways to us. May we faithfully do our part as the Lord continues to do His.

Application

Read: 1 Thessalonians 5:5-8

Pray: Ask God to help you stay alert to situations and thoughts that come to you each day. Ask Him for peace no matter what happens.

Reflect: In what areas do you feel you need to be more spiritually alert? List them, and then determine to stay alert by reading the Word and praying about them.

Day 28 - <u>Once is Enough</u>

And Stephen, full of faith and power, did great wonders and miracles among the people. And they were not able to resist the wisdom and the spirit by which he spake. Acts 6:8, 10

I once read about a minister who kept preaching the same sermon week after week. When asked why he said that he would keep preaching the same sermon until people started living out the message he was trying to get across.

After reading this, at first I thought that the people he was preaching to must be either hard of hearing or spiritually dead. Or perhaps he was preaching the wrong sermon. Then I thought of the convicting sermons the apostles of the Book of Acts preached, which were so potent people immediately reacted. Either they repented and were converted or they were so angry they wanted the apostles dead for creating such a stir that required they change their heart and their way of living. Steven preached a sermon that cost him his life. In fact, I believe all of the apostles who preached in the same way (with power and conviction of the Holy Spirit) were martyred for preaching the convicting and life-giving message of the Gospel.

While there is no substitute for personal daily prayer and Bible devotions, still, we like to hear sermons that leave a lasting impression. In fact, if I was to think back and try to remember the sermons I've heard in a local church, very few really stayed with me and created a change in my heart and life. I've often wondered why this is. I believe that a person goes to church to receive from God and to grow in one's faith. But in order to receive from God, a minister needs to have really listened to the Lord's leading and also be willing to preach the sermon God gives, even if it doesn't fit a pre-planned agenda or series of sermons that a minister may have chosen even months ahead of time.

Day 28

It takes a lot of courage to speak the truth of God's Word to people who may be less than willing to receive it. It may mean a loss of numbers when people quit coming to church. Or it may mean a much stronger church, as less serious believers are weeded out from those who mean business with God. I have seen anointed ministers more than once get up to preach, then share that the Lord had impressed on them to preach a different sermon. These sermons were timely, convicting, and specific to the needs of the congregation for that particular time. The Lord never makes a mistake. What we think we need to hear is sometimes not what God had ever intended for that particular time.

We must discern also what is from God and what is not. Many sermons have left me feeling confused, guilty and almost depressed. Rather than life-giving, they seemed to drag me down and left me feeling discouraged. This is not the Lord's way. When His Word goes forth, it goes with a defined purpose and brings "living" and tangible results and seeks to build us up rather than tear us down (see Acts 20:32). Also, rather than try to change people by repeating the same sermon over and over again, God's Word will do the changing as Scripture promises (see Hebrews 4:12). May we continue to pray for our ministers that they follow the specific leading of the Lord when it comes to preaching sermons.

Application

Read: Acts 6

Pray: for your minister that he or she will be open to God's leading and preach sermons inspired by God. Pray that you will always be open to God's leading in your own life.

Reflect: Think back on a sermon that you never forgot. If possible, write that minister and tell him or her how their sermon impacted your life.

Day 29 - <u>Giants in the Land</u>

And Caleb stilled the people before Moses, and said, Let us go up at once, and possess it; for we are well able to overcome it. But the men that went up with him said, We be not able to go up against the people; for they are stronger than we. Numbers 13:30-31

When my husband and I purchased our condo, we had made a list of things we would do to renovate it. We had calculated the costs and felt confident it was all within our budget. But soon, we discovered there were other things that we didn't know about that would need our immediate attention. We had bought the condo with five appliances, so were pleased we wouldn't have to purchase these big items. But we found that the stove didn't work, so we had to bring the one from our house which was new, which would now leave us without a stove at our summer residence. Then we found that the washing machine didn't work, so we had to purchase a brand new one for the condo. About a week later, we got a phone call from the manager telling us that there was a leak in our plumbing under the kitchen sink that had affected the owners below us, so we couldn't use the dishwasher and would have to get a plumber in, who would also have to fix the upstairs shower which didn't work properly. Then we discovered a problem with the electrical and had to have an electrician come in and fix our wall heater in our bedroom.

My husband and I both agreed that each of these situations seemed like giants to us. We hadn't in any way factored in these extra costs that would have to be attended to. Where would we get the money? We had already spent any left-over money for renovations. In spite of these unexpected expenses, we believe that God gave us this condo to live in and enjoy and which would also give my husband a much shorter drive to and from work. So we believed that in each situation, God was wanting to show us

Day 29

that while these things appear as giants, we are to boldly move forward in the strength, power and confidence of the Lord even with no extra financial resources seemingly available.

I am not surprised that we are often under such fiery trials. As Christians and ministers of the Gospel, we are an immediate threat to our enemy Satan, especially if the area we live in is spiritually dark. He does not want us coming in, as Caleb did, and go in to possess the land for God. He wants us to cower and retreat, give up and admit defeat when we see the bigness of our problems and what we are up against. He hopes we will be discouraged and focus on the problems rather than focus on our God and our goal to go in and possess the land for Him.

Problems are like a boat with holes. You plug one hole and pretty soon another one pops up and you have to plug that one too. Life is like that. Problems will always present themselves, whether they are financial, health concerns, relationship troubles or any number of other things. This life will never be perfect. So we have a choice. Either we will move forward to defeat the giants in our way through the action of prayer and faith, or we will give in to defeat and allow the problems to bury us in discouragement and fear. May we choose to move forward, focusing on our main goal — to go in and possess the land for Him.

Application

Read: Numbers 13:17-33

Pray: If you are facing giants in your life, ask the Lord to take care of them for you; then go in to possess the land for God.

Reflect: What are some giants you need to overcome? Resolve to take action and do the work of the Lord in spite of them.

Day 30 - <u>Confidence</u>

Being confident of this very thing, that he which hath begun a good work in you will perform it until the day of Jesus Christ: Philippians 1:6

If you were to think back to your childhood, what was the first thing you remember doing well and that gave you confidence? For me, I remember when I was nine years old and my parents gave me my first two-wheel bicycle. I had outgrown my tricycle and my sister had been given a two-wheel bike with training wheels from my great Uncle Alf. It was a birthday gift, even though my birthday wasn't until late December. The first time I rode it, it was pretty high up and I fell on the gravel driveway leaving scars on my knees that would last most of my childhood and teenage years. But pretty soon, I got the hang of it and I'd ride my bike everywhere, all over the neighbourhood, to school and beyond. When you're a kid and you don't have a car or any way to get around except walk and run, a bike opens up a whole new world for you. I am glad that I continued to ride my bike even after taking such a hard fall that first day. I still ride a bike and it is one of the most enjoyable outdoor activities I know of.

Often there are things we want to pursue or do, but we just lack the confidence. After I was involved in a head-on car collision (as a passenger) when I was a teenager, I vowed I would never drive even when I turned 16 and would be legally able to. But my dad insisted I try. So I did and he even bought me my first car, which I was glad to get especially when I moved away from home right after graduation and would need it to get me from the boarding house I was staying in to the college nearby. There are many other things I've lacked confidence in because of fear or because I may have failed the first few times. But by continuing to try, it gave me courage to try more difficult challenges further along the way. Learning how to paint gave

Day 30

me confidence to attempt to do a wall mural in a resort town close to our summer cottage, even though I just began with pencil sketchings, then small watercolor paintings and then finally full-blown acrylic paintings. Yet, at one time, I would never have imagined myself as an artist. I just loved doodling. You never know what a simple thing like doodling can lead to. For someone else, maybe they like cooking, or woodworking. Cooking, even simple things, can lead to making delicious gourmet meals.

But there is another confidence that we all need — and that is to know that our spiritual lives are progressively improving and that we are getting somewhere. How do we know if we are progressing when it comes to spiritual matters? We may think it has to do with how many good works we perform, how often we go to church and how much we give and tithe. These are all good things, but they will not make us any more righteous. Even if we do as many good works as we can think of, still, only the Lord knows what constitutes good and He knows how far we've come and how far we still need to go. I like the opening verse: *he which hath begun a good work in you will perform it.* This is indeed good news — we don't have to strive to be righteous, but our confidence lies in the work of the Lord Jesus Christ and He will be faithful to perfect us in His own way and time.

Application

<u>Read</u>: Ephesians 2:8-10

<u>Pray</u>: **Thank God for the good work He is doing in your life. Spend time with Him praising Him for all your many accomplishments.**

<u>Reflect</u>: **What are some of your main accomplishments? What would you like to try that you have never tried before? Try it today!**

Day 31 - <u>What Kind of Memories?</u>

Remember his marvellous works that he hath done; his wonders, and the judgments of his mouth; Psalm 105:5

Have you ever thought about what you would like to be remembered for? I have often read obituaries just to see what a person did with their life. I have attended many funerals over the years and have often written an encouraging poem or inspirational message to try and comfort those mourning the loss of their loved one. Sometimes memories of people are easier to write about than others because of their kindnesses that are never forgotten. The importance of leaving behind the warmest memories for our loved ones to cherish might be something we overlook completely, but still it is well worth cultivating. Somehow it makes the grieving easier to bear.

Has anyone ever done anything for you that you never forgot? I have memories of my uncle bringing me back souvenirs from his trips to the United States. Another uncle gave me a little porcelain Siamese cat ornament that I still have. I have a prominent memory of my mother coming to my rescue when I couldn't make the monthly payments on my new car when I was only working part time. She worked hard for her money and she was saving it for new and badly needed flooring. There are some people that you could never think a bad thought about no matter how hard you try. These are the people who will be remembered for their kindnesses long after they are gone from this life. My mother is one of those people, always giving and thinking of others.

In the opening verse we have a reminder to remember the works of God. How easy it is to forget Who He is and all that He's done for us especially in our busy and often complicated lives. We may skip reading the Bible and praying

Day 31

altogether, and so forget all the wonderful aspects of a God who loves us and wants us to know Him. The psalmist David wrote: I remember the days of old; I meditate on all thy works; I muse on the work of thy hands (Psalm 143:5). If we were to meditate on all the many kindnesses that the Lord has done for us, they would likely be too many to count. We may remember when we first heard the Gospel and responded. I remember how the Lord set me free from a life of slavery to sin and tell about it to this day. We may remember times He provided a much needed job, or unexpected money arrived in the mail. We may remember times He has healed us and other times He has provided us with a new friend or fellowship in our times of aloneness. Or we may remember someone who came to us when they felt led to do so and met a specific need that only God knew about. Maybe we ourselves have been conduits of God's grace, mercy and provision. These are the kinds of memories to dwell on. These are the kinds of things we want to be remembered for.

So why not do something out of the ordinary for someone? In fact do something extraordinary that will stretch us in some way and provide a nice memory of us for someone after we're gone? Better yet, do something that will draw someone closer to God.

Application

Read: Psalm 105:1-8

Pray: Ask God to bring to your mind wonderful memories of what He's done for you. Trust Him to continue to provide for all of your needs.

Reflect: Take time to meditate and recall the goodness of God in your life. Make a resolve to create good memories for others to remember you by.

An Invitation for Salvation

Dear Friend,

I hope this book has encouraged you. Daily devotions only truly benefit us once we've given our heart and entire life over to the Lord Jesus Christ. If you would like to receive Jesus into your heart and life today, and also have the assurance that you will spend eternity in heaven with Him, please begin by saying this prayer:

Dear Heavenly Father,

I come to you in the name of Jesus. Your Word says, "Whosoever shall call upon the name of the Lord shall be saved" (Acts 2:21). I call on you now and ask Jesus to come into my heart, forgive me for all my sins, and cleanse me. I ask you to be Lord over my life according to Romans 10:9-10 — "That if thou shalt confess with thy mouth the Lord Jesus, and shalt believe in thine heart that God hath raised him from the dead, thou shalt be saved. For with the heart man believeth unto righteousness; and with the mouth confession is made unto salvation." I do this now — I confess that Jesus is Lord and I believe in my heart that God raised Him from the dead.

In Jesus Name,
Amen

You are now reborn! You are a Christian and a child of God! Be assured, you have taken the most important step of your life and God has reserved your place in heaven. He will always be with you and lead you into all truth (read Hebrews 13:5b; John 14:26). You will need to read the Bible on a daily basis to get to know Him and all the many promises He has for you. As well, don't delay in contacting a Bible-believing church where you will find fellowship with others who have also taken this important life-changing step. May God bless you as you continue on your new path of life and freedom in Christ!

About the Author

Linda McBurney-Gunhouse enjoys her life in Manitoba, Canada. She writes to help others and inspire them to overcome difficulties and achieve success in life. She also enjoys story-telling in the form of writing fiction. Linda has spent a life-time writing and honing her skills. She studied Journalism, English, and History and received both a BA and B.Ed. in English. She has a diploma in magazine writing. She has worked as a contributing editor for a community college and also as an editor for a community newspaper in Winnipeg. Her articles have appeared in national, city and community newspapers and one magazine. She has written and sold one radio play. She is an accomplished eBook author of several inspirational books, including five full-length fiction. Her readership is international, and some of her eBooks frequently reach the Top 100 in specific categories. Linda also writes thought-provoking blogs.

She loves to share her faith and how she has overcome the many challenges in life in a way that readers can relate to. She sometimes teaches Creative Writing, and she does special speaking. She sometimes does free-lance writing for the local newspapers. She has also facilitated her own writer's group in a local setting. She continues to expand her thought-provoking blogs and book-writing. When she is not writing, she loves to be involved in creating several mediums of art.

Other Titles by Linda McBurney-Gunhouse

Inspirational Books

When Love Is All There Is
Loneliness: The Pathway to Discovery
Victory Over Backsliding
Footpath to Freedom
The Journey of Oneness
Power Thoughts for Positive Thinking
The Power of Submission
Healing For The Wounded Soul
The Act of Decision-Making
Cures for Stress
Freedom Through Spiritual Discernment
Spiritual Leadership in a Fallen World
The Journey to Contentment
No Fear of Hell
Money: Master or Servant?
The Bible: Conformed or Transformed?
Healing & Hope for Child Loss
Essential Steps to Increase Your Faith
Making Sense of the Rapture

Biography

The Bonk Saga: A History of Memories
Called to Overcome

Other Titles

Devotionals

Pathways to Devotion I
Pathways to Devotion II
Pathways to Devotion III
Pathways to Devotion IV
Pathways to Devotion V
Pathways to Devotion VI
Pathways to Devotion VII
Pathways to Devotion VIII
Pathways to Devotion IX
Pathways to Devotion X
Pathways to Devotion XI

Fiction

The Redemption of Steep Rock Cove
Return to Steep Rock Cove
Christmas Comes to Steep Rock Cove
Waves of Change at Steep Rock Cove
Driving with the Top Down
Track Three

Poetry Books

Heart Songs
Songs in the Desert
Water Crossings
Wings I: Morning Arising
Wings II: Daylight Reflections
Wings III: Contemplation

Other Titles

Creative How-to Books

Artistic Ideas & Inspirations
How to Create Stories From Your Own Life
Living a Creative Life

Writing Manuals

Creative Writing
Write Your Life Story
Fiction Writing

Please visit our website at www.creativefocus.ca to discover the many books from this list that are available as eBooks.

Note: If you have enjoyed reading this book, or any other eBook of mine, please rate it online, or recommend it on your Facebook page. It will help spread the word, and let others know it is available. My goal is to help, encourage and inspire others through my writing. Thank you and may God richly bless you!